*Laughing in Lee*

Mission Point Press
2554 Chandler Road
Traverse City, Michigan 49696
www.MissionPointPress.com
231-421-9513

ISBN: 978-1-950659-51-7
Library of Congress Control Number: 2020906597

Printed in the United States of America

# LAUGHING IN LEELANAU
## OR, I SWEAR IT'S TRUE

## By SCOTT CRAIG
### Illustrated by Henry Coleman

**MISSION POINT PRESS**

FOR CAROL, JENNIFER, AND AMY
*whose laughter is the joy of my life*

"A little nonsense now and then,
is relished by the wisest men."
—*Roald Dahl*

"Everything is funny as long as it's happening to
someone else …. Live in such a way that you would
not be ashamed to sell your parrot to the town gossip."
—*Will Rogers*

# Contents

Clip joints • 16

Miscellany • 21

Key moments • 22

"Suttons Bay, MI" (song) • 28

Fudgies • 30

Miscellany too • 38

"Kerosene, camphor and lard" • 41

The crossing • 42

Fishtown • 44

"Carp River Blues" (song) • 50

Percy • 51

More miscellany • 55

The tip of the tip • 57

"A Little Town Called Northport" (song) • 57

Miscellany again • 64

Animal crackers • 65

Oh! Men!! Ahhh • 80

"Ode to Omena" (song) • 81

The Petoskey • 85

Miscellany once more • 87

"A Song of Glen Lake" • 90

The runaway • 91

John Barleycorn • 92

The poet • 97

Miscellany also • 102

By the bay • 104

Earl the pearl • 107

The three r's • 112

The jokester • 114

The sporting life • 118

"Wearin' of the Green" (poem) • 119

Angling • 121

Cream or sugar? • 128

Miscellany encore • 130

Fire! Fire! • 132

The long arm of the law • 135

The hoosegow • 140

Ultimate wisdom • 146

"I'm Going Back to Leelanau" (song) • 147

About the author and illustrator • 150

Leelanau County

Traverse City

Lake Huron

Lake Michigan

Lansing

Detroit

Chicago

I belong to a small breakfast club that gathers weekly year-round at Trish's Dishes, a friendly cafe in the village of Leland, Michigan. One lovely, early northern morning, a member of our group, Logan Hardy, showed up with a broad grin on his face. He had gone to college in Maine and could, when he chose, speak with a Maine accent. In his hand was a copy of a small book entitled "Maine Humor." For the next ten minutes or so he regaled us with folksy Down East tales. You know what I mean … "You can't get there from here," and so on. As I listened, a thought struck me. "I think I can put together that kind of thing. We've got plenty of our own funny stuff right here in Leelanau County." I was encouraged when, during my later quest for northern humor, I met with Tim Barr, owner of Art's Tavern in Glen Arbor. He told me, "No, I never say that 'You can't get there from here' stuff. I just tell a confused tourist, 'I think you are so completely screwed up, you should go back home and start over.'"

Since the time the idea popped into my head, I have talked to well over a hundred folks in this county, attended a number of local coffee clubs, sought help from Kim Kelderhouse at the Leelanau Historical Society, and pored over years of issues of the *Leelanau Enterprise*. I am most grateful. This experience has proven to be one of the most wonderful times of my life.

Some say the name of our county was derived from the French words "lee," which means protective shelter, and "eau" for water. Others contend it was named by Henry Schoolcraft in 1840, who said it meant "delight of life." The county's Chamber of Commerce adopted Schoolcraft's version, officially promoting it as "The Land of Delight."

Leelanau is surrounded on three sides by Lake Michigan — a peninsula on a peninsula. It includes five Lake Michigan islands, the largest of which are North and South Manitou. The county sits astride the 45th Parallel, providing an ideal climate for the growing of fruit, particularly cherries. We also produce peaches, plums, pears, apples, strawberries and grapes. We have more than 30 wineries in Leelanau. There are 43 lakes within its borders. The largest, Lake Leelanau, runs through the middle. The famous road M22 pretty much circles the county following the lakeshore. We have only one stoplight, no fast-food restaurants, and no franchise hotels. Sleeping Bear National Lakeshore, located on the west side of the county, was named "The Most Beautiful Place in the Nation" by *Good Morning America* in 2011.

Today there are slightly over twenty thousand souls living year-round in Leelanau County. (In the summer months the population soars to many times that.) The largest town is Greilickville on the southern edge. Suttons Bay is the county seat and the business hub. To the north is Peshawbestown, the tribal center of government for the Grand Traverse Band of Ottawa and Chippewa Indians. Other villages that figure prominently in the county are Northport, Cedar, Empire, Glen Arbor, Glen Haven, Leland, Maple City — and Lake

Leelanau. Yes, not only is there a body of water with that name, there is a small village as well. And that is where things can get confusing.

So, let me attempt to clarify. There is a hamlet at the "narrows" between the north and south sections of the watery Lake Leelanau. The town was originally called "Provemont." However, in 1924, the residents, for their own reasons, decided to change the name. As a result, there is now a town on Lake Leelanau named "Lake Leelanau." To complicate matters even more, the original name for that body of water was Carp Lake. As the area grew in popularity, residents decided tourists would not be drawn to a lake named after an ugly fish. So, they changed it. Likewise, the outlet of the lake that drains into Lake Michigan was named Carp River. That moniker was dropped in favor of the "Leland River." Therefore, in coming pages, when dealing with historical material, if you see "Provemont," it's today's town of Lake Leelanau. "Carp Lake" is the body of water now called "Lake Leelanau," and the "Carp River" is really the "Leland River." I know this is mind-boggling, yet residents of the county accept the potential confusion, knowing some other things here can be quite logical, like the signs that appear with some regularity reading "Road Ends at the Water." Of course it does.

The towns of Leelanau County are quite independent, fiercely defending their identities. Once, while attending the Leland International Coffee Club, I remarked that the woman leading our exercise class was a "local." Bruce Price, one of the county's great pundits, responded with conviction, "She's not a 'local.' She's from Cedar!" There are currently four different public-school districts and several private and religious schools. Only once in our modern history was there a consolidation. That happened after much controversy in the late '50s. My friend Fred Atkinson, a retired school superintendent, clarified the issue best when he asked me, "Do you know what is the hardest animal in the whole world to kill?" His answer, "A high school mascot."

# Clip joints

One of the early barber shops in Leelanau County was Bert Russel's in Northport. At the beginning of the last century, one could get a shave there for 15 cents and a haircut for a quarter. In 1917, Bert installed a bathtub in an adjacent room. It was special, being the third one in the village. Water was heated over a wood fire. A bath cost 25 cents if you brought your own towel, 35 cents if the towel was furnished by the shop. Bert proudly advertised that after each bath, his son even cleaned out the tub.

**Leelanau Enterprise**, April 1921

"Dr. Ruff took a German bath last week. He says it was the first he's taken in six months."

Kathy Firestone told me that for several years, on Halloween night, boys in Northport plopped a stolen outhouse in front of Russel's Barber Shop. No one remembers exactly why they always chose that location. It apparently just seemed funny to them. Town fathers tried with no avail to stop the practice. Kathy said it only ended when Northport ran out of privies.

Today there are two traditional barber shops in the county. The better-known is Jon's in Suttons Bay. Beginning in 1965, Jon Smith, the shop's owner, held forth in the barber chair beside the west window. He's retired now, and his son Chip has taken over his spot. Mike, Kurt, and Paul are behind the other chairs. There could not be a more affable bunch. They are skilled cutters of hair, easy with chatter, and keen observers of the world that passes through their door.

One day, a little boy was next in turn for his haircut at Jon's. Mike put a board across the arms of his chair to accommodate the lad. "My, you're certainly growing up," Mike remarked. The boy replied, "Yes, I'm five years old. (pause) Going into first grade next year. (pause-sigh) You know, at this point of my life, time passes very quickly."

Because they are so widely known in the county, the barbers at Jon's take a bunch of good-natured ridicule. Mary Stanton says one time when she was in Dot's Bakery in Northport, she overheard a man telling his buddy that he was on his way to Jon's. "I'm going to tell him to cut my hair two inches above my ear on the right side. On the left, I want my hair to hang below the ear. I'm going to tell him to leave the back full and I want him to take a few random whacks at the front." "Why in the world would you tell him that?" his friend asked. "Consistency," was the reply. "That's the way he cut it the last time."

The story goes that a body of a man was found by police in Brooklyn. There was no identification on him. The police were baffled until a detective spoke up. "Well, we do have one clue," he announced. "He got his hair cut in Suttons Bay, Michigan."

Northport's Ray Kellogg settled into Jon's chair and said, "Since I'm bald, I think you should charge me less." "On the contrary," Jon replied. "I'm charging you more, because what hair you have left is so hard to find."

⤚

Jon's Barber Shop is unique in that it is also a sporting goods store. You can get your hunting and fishing licenses there. They sell all kinds of fishing gear, air rifles, knives and ammunition. They also sell bait — worms, crawlers, and sometimes wigglers. What is a wiggler, you ask? Well, it's the larval stage of the mayfly. At certain times of the year, they can be found by anglers who dig them out of the mud on riverbanks. They look like a hideously ugly centipede, but fish love them. The writer Bill Crandell recounts the story about a customer who was drinking a cup of coffee while waiting for his haircut. It was at the time when Jon was still presiding over the shop. The customer got up to go to the restroom, placing his cup beside the cash register just as Jon was selling a box of wigglers to a fisherman. The customer returned, retrieved his coffee, and sat back down. A few minutes later, he jumped from his chair and screamed, "My God! There's a wiggler in the bottom of my cup!" To which Jon replied, "I wonder what happened to the other one?"

﹏

There was a time when Jon had a pressing problem. He had bought a new snowmobile, a very pricey one. In fact, it was so expensive that he didn't know how to tell his wife about it. So, he had hidden it in the shed. One afternoon, while having beers at Eddie's Tavern in Suttons Bay, he shared his dilemma with some of his pals. During the conversation, he mentioned that he and his wife were going out for dinner that evening. After he left, his pals decided to help him out with the problem. When Jon and his wife came home from their night out, he turned on the light to discover, sitting on his dining room table, his snowmobile! The jig was up! Instead of getting angry, Jon said, "You know, I've got to start thinking about locking the doors."

# Miscellany

**Leelanau Enterprise** advertisement,
February 1924

The All Year Car For Every Family

Chevrolet

Two Passenger Roadster — $510

Four Passenger Touring Car — $525

**Leelanau Enterprise**, March 6, 1924

"Automobiles are now nearly foolproof, but their drivers are not."

# Key moments

Jon Smith's mother lived in the tiny village of Omena for many years. Her home was directly across the road from the bar. In her later years, she began telling friends that she thought she might be losing her mind. She could swear she had certain items of groceries, but when she'd look for them, they were nowhere to be found. She told the story often enough that family members really began to worry about her. Then one night when it was very late, she thought she heard a noise downstairs. She slipped on a robe and tip-toed to the kitchen. There at the table, was an inebriated man eating a snack! The bar had closed at 2 a.m. and he was hungry. It turned out that for years he'd been a late-night dining regular in her kitchen. Yet he was fastidious, leaving no clues behind. He'd carefully clean up the kitchen every night before weaving back through the door. Jon's mother told the family that perhaps she, too, might start thinking about locking her doors.

It's a fact that lots of folks in Leelanau feel so secure that, like Jon and his mother, they don't bother to lock their doors. (Because I'm now making this public, that practice may change ... but I doubt it.) In fact, realtor Tim Schaub told me that quite often the last obstacle in closing the sale of the house is when the old owner can't find the key.

In Bill Carlson's Leland boyhood home, the family bedrooms were upstairs, with a sole guest bedroom on the ground floor. One early morning, Bill came downstairs and noticed the front door standing wide open. Next, he heard what sounded like a snore coming from the guest room. He went in to find a man asleep in the bed. Bill shook him awake and demanded, "What are you doing here?" "What do you mean?" the guy responded sleepily. "I have every right to be here. This is my house!" "Where do you live?" Bill asked. "Second Street," came the reply. "Well, this is First Street," Bill responded. "Get out of here and go home."

～

Beth Grosvenor was making breakfast when, to her surprise, a man entered the kitchen by way of the basement stairs. Beth screamed for her husband, "Mike! Mike!" The stranger was puzzled. He had been at the Bluebird the night before and had decided it wouldn't be wise to drive home. Someone at the bar volunteered to let him stay at his house and provided the address. He said, "Just go on in. The door is unlocked." The stranger, it turned out, was not good at remembering details like addresses. So, he entered a home with an unlocked door and mistakenly spent the night in the Grosvenors' basement on grandma's old couch.

～

Bahle's Department Store has been a family-run business in Suttons Bay since 1876. Today it primarily sells clothing, but in the old days its stock was more diversified, including appliances. Lois Bahle remembers being sent by her father to deliver a new refrigerator to a home on North Lake Street in Leland. When she and a helper got there, no one was at home. They had been told that might be the case so, because the door was unlocked, they wrestled the new appliance into the house. Once there, they discovered that the existing refrigerator in the kitchen was full of food. It certainly didn't look like it had been prepared for a removal. Lois rechecked the address and realized that the delivery was supposed to occur on South Lake Street, not North. So, they retrieved the new refrigerator and drove to the right address. No one was home there either and, as expected, the door there too, was unlocked. All's well that ends well.

و

Phil Deering of Empire says, "You can always tell the new people in town. They lock their cars."

و

Will Case-Daniels and his wife lived in the northern part of the county. It was a pleasant little neighborhood, except for one thing. The man living next door had a drinking problem. On one occasion, Will had house guests, two guys he knew from Missouri who were spending a few days taking in the sights. Will and his wife were getting ready to go out to a party. Their guests were just going to hang out at home. Will's wife had just finished dressing when the neighbor, with a "load on," wobbled through Will's unlocked front door and into the bedroom scaring Will's wife and passing out on the floor! Running a bit late for the party, Will called on his Missouri friends for help. "Would you guys please carry this fellow next door and put him to bed?" he asked. His pals followed instructions and returned. As Will was leaving, something a guest had said made him pause. "Did you take him to the house to the north or the one to the south?" he asked. "To the north," came the answer. "Oh, God," said Will. "That's the wrong 'next door'! Get him out of there and put him to bed in the other one." The Missourians accomplished the task with ease, since neither house was locked.

⁓

Suttons Bay's Bill Klein opened his garage and discovered a cigarette butt on the floor. It bothered him because no one in the family smoked. He decided he should start locking the garage door, and he did — for a couple of days.

⁓

For years, Phil Deering kept an old pickup truck parked beside his grocery store in Empire. Of course, the keys were always in it. From time to time, his wife would give him a stern warning about the practice. "Someone is going to steal it," she told him. But Phil is an easygoing guy, and it was simpler not to change. He also let just about anybody borrow the truck who asked. "The keys are in the ignition," he'd tell them. One day, a man named George took the vehicle but forgot to ask Phil. He also forgot to bring it back. Phil noticed the next morning that the truck was missing. By asking around, he determined it was indeed George who had the truck. Phil certainly couldn't ask his wife to drive him out to George's farm, so he walked the three miles to retrieve it. I wondered if that experience would persuade him to stop the practice of leaving the keys in the truck. "Why would I do that?" he replied incredulously.

‎ﺑ‎

Bill Klein remembers a time when officials from the state were coming to Suttons Bay for a meeting about a harbor issue. It was to be held in the evening at the bank. Participants gathered on the sidewalk at the appointed hour, only to discover the door was locked. "No, problem," said the banker, as he reached above the frame, grabbed the key from the transom, and let them in.

*Suttons Bay, Mich.*

Words by L.G. Herbert
Tune: "Jingle Bells"
(undated)

It's Sutton Bay for me,
To her I will be true.
I'll whoop it up for my hometown.
Her good I will pursue.
I'll boost her far and wide,
I'll sing her worthy praise,
I'll stand by her whate'er betide,
For her my song I'll raise.

CHORUS:
Sutton Bay, Suttons Bay
Suttons Bay, Hoorah!
I'll boost her everywhere I go,
I'll boost her every day.
Suttons Bay, Suttons Bay,
Suttons Bay on tap.
We're coming, coming on the run,
The best town on the map!

## Leelanau Enterprise, July 1895

"A small party of Leland people went on an excursion on Carp Lake aboard the steamer Wiggler on last Sunday. After coasting along the shore of the lake for some time, they discovered a party of campers who had set up quarters in a small grove near Bingham. The interest of the passengers was so aroused that the boat was brought to a stop and a man sent ashore to get information about the camp. He was informed it was Camp Tired, and the campers were certainly the most tired looking lot he had seen in many a day. The only camper fully alive informed the man from the boat that the entire camp would return to the city in the morning to take a rest."

# Fudgies

In different parts of the United States, locals have coined nicknames for tourists. In Colorado they are called "Flat Landers," in New England "Cone Lickers," in Florida "Q Tips" because of their white hair and white tennis shoes, in Wisconsin "Shackers" because they rent cabins, and in Maine "Cidiots" for obvious reasons. In Northern Michigan, they are known as "Fudgies." The name seems to have originated on Mackinac Island where there are numerous fudge shops. Somewhere in the distant past, tourists carrying little white bags filled with fudge acquired the label. As time passed, fudge shops opened across the northern part of the state, Leelanau County included. Without fudgies, our economy would tank, so we appreciate them, as well as the humor they provide.

❧

Tad McKay, who once owned the classy gift shop The Tin Soldier in Leland, remembers when a woman came into his store, pointed west toward the water, and asked, "Is that the Atlantic or the Pacific?"

Charter fishing captain Jack Duffy had taken a client out and set lines just off North Manitou Island. The client asked, "Tell me, where exactly is Lake Michigan?" Jack replied, "If you fall overboard, you'll find out."

Mike Grosvenor, whose family has owned the Manitou Island Transit ferry since 1913, remembers a fudgie asking him, "How far is it to South Manitou Island?" "Seventeen miles," he replied. "Oh," said the fudgie, "then how far is it back?"

A fudgie asked Lois Bahle of Suttons Bay, "Is the water as high here on Grand Traverse Bay as it is in Lake Michigan?"

My brother Rob Craig and his wife Sharon were in the Synchronicity Gallery in Glen Arbor. They observed a woman who had just selected two beautiful and rather expensive paintings. The clerk asked if she should prepare the bill. The woman answered, "Wait. I need to go out to the car and ask Old Yahwhadever." "Who's that?" asked the puzzled clerk. "My husband," replied the lady. "I'm going out to the car and ask if it's all right to buy two paintings, and he'll say, 'Yah. Whatever.'"

‿

"I'M SO GLAD TO SEE THE FUDGIES BACK.
I HAVE'NT SNARLED AT ANYBODY SINCE LAST SEPTEMBER."

‿

FUDGIE TO MIKE GROSVENOR: HOW
MANY DOES YOUR FERRY BOAT HOLD?

MIKE: OUR MAXIMUM IS 136.

FUDGIE: PEOPLE?

～

Piper Goldson owns and operates the Suttons Bay
Gallery. She selects her pieces with great expertise.
The collection contains paintings and prints from
the masters as well as some of the world's finest
contemporary artists. A fudgie spent a long time
looking at the works and then remarked to her
with great admiration, "Boy, you got some guys
up here in Michigan that really know how to draw
pictures!"

～

Piper's husband Harry is quite a successful invest-
ment banker. However, in his youth, he played the
clarinet in some of our nation's most famous Big
Bands. He still likes to play professionally from
time to time, and his musical artistry is magical.
For a few years, he and Piper organized the popular Suttons Bay Jazz Festival. One time, after a
performance, a woman approached him. "Mr.
Goldson," she asked, "Was that jazz, or were you
just making that up?"

A group of Northport pals took a fudgie friend for a sail through the Straits of Mackinac. The fudgie was at the helm and saw the giant bridge looming up about eight miles ahead. From that distance, the span looked quite close to the water. One of the friends told him to call ahead to get the bridge raised so they could pass through. The fudgie did as told and the answering official (who had received this kind of request before) said, "When you get about a mile away, call me again and we'll raise her for you."

My son-in-law, Neil Coleman, was relaxing on the sand by Lake Michigan with a friend, a first-time visitor from Los Angeles. There was a commotion down the beach. A man had gotten into trouble in the water and friends had rescued him. A crowd gathered. Neil's friend asked, "Was that a shark attack?" "No," answered Neil. "These waters are perfectly safe. There are no sharks in here." With a superior look on his face, his friend replied, "That's what they always say in Los Angeles too."

Kim Kelderhouse of the Leelanau Historical Society was giving a tour of the old abandoned South Manitou lighthouse. She pointed up to the tower and said that the lamp up there was once powered by kerosene, but in the very old days, they used whale oil. A woman in the group asked, "Where is the best place to go whale watching on Lake Michigan?"

Shortly after Mike and Mary Fleishman moved to Leland, they were working in the garden of their home. Their next-door neighbor, Willa Bokstahler, stopped by for a chat. She had lived in Leland for most of her life so is a full-blooded "local." Mike asked her, "How long does it take for us to escape from the term 'fudgie'?" "Oh, you already have," she answered. "Fudgies don't do their own yard work."

Over the years, the bar at the Bluebird in Leland has been the site of many weighty debates and the source of numerous earth-shaking pronouncements. One evening, the subject of fudgies came up. The question was, "What do you call an out-of-towner who comes north in the winter to ski, skate, or snowshoe?" After lengthy discussion, it was determined they should be called "fudge-sicles." Then another problem of semantics arose. We all knew what a "fudgie" was and we all knew what a "local" was. But what about those of us who weren't born here but had property in Leelanau County and spent lots of time here? What were we? After much speculation, it was decided that we were "perma-fudge."

# Miscellany too

**Leelanau Enterprise** advertisement,
Nov. 13, 1930

ANNUAL TURKEY DAY

Gronseth's Shoe Store

Suttons Bay, Michigan

Saturday, Nov. 22

3:00 PM

Two large turkeys will be thrown
from the roof of our store.
They are yours for the catching.

**Leelanau Enterprise**, September 1885

"Dr. James Brady, Leland's leading physician and surgeon, is having a new foundation built under his house since the old one has become so dangerously shaky no one will call at his place of business."

ے

**Leelanau Enterprise**, April 25, 1893

"Everyone knows that cod liver oil has a very disagreeable taste. The pleasantest way to take it is to fatten your pigeons with it and then eat the pigeons."

ے

## Kerosene, camphor and lard

By Harry R. Dumbrille
The Poet of Leelanau, 1927

When I was a lad,
I used to choke up
With a cold and be
Hoarse as a crow;
I'd jump out of bed,
In the room overhead,
And yell at my folks down below.

My mother would come,
As soon as she could,
With some kerosene,
Camphor and lard;
She'd just do her best,
To soak up my chest
With the mixture,
And rub it in hard.

To those who have colds,
I would just like to say,
(And I'd say the same
Thing to my pard.)
Just rub up your chests
In the old-fashioned way,
With some kerosene,
Camphor, and lard.

# The crossing

As I said, North and South Manitou Islands are a part of Leelanau County as well as being a portion of the Sleeping Bear National Lakeshore. Both islands are uninhabited. Campers and hikers get to them by way of a ferry service, the Manitou Island Transit, which operates out of Leland. South Manitou is seventeen miles from Leland while North is twelve. The northern island is the larger at eight miles long and four miles wide. The islands were the first part of Leelanau County to be settled in the mid-19th century. That's partially because they were easily reached by water. Early settlers made their livings fishing, farming, and selling cord wood to passing steamships.

Nels Carlson and his family arrived on North Manitou sometime in the 1870s. They were of both Swedish and Norwegian ancestry. After a couple of decades of farming, Nels determined it was time to move to the mainland where roads had now been built and there was more opportunity. On March 17, 1903, the family started across the ice. There were eleven of them. They had packed their belongings onto three large logging sledges pulled by oxen. Nels made sure there was an adult male on each in case of trouble. The sledges were positioned a mile apart to spread out the weight on the ice.

The going was slow. From time to time, jarring cracking sounds were heard. It took the Carlsons nine hours to cover the 12 miles to Leland, but they did — arriving safe and sound. The next morning, Nels went outside to look around. What he saw provoked surprise, horror, and relief. The wind had shifted during the night and Lake Michigan, between Leland and its islands, was totally open water.

Now, there is nothing particularly funny about that story. It simply has a happy outcome. I guarantee that in this book you'll find no unhappy endings.

Today, the harbor area of Leland is anchored by the Carlson Fishery. It is owned by a fifth-generation member of this Leelanau County family, who is named for his great-great-grandfather, Nels.

# Fishtown

In the heart of the village of Leland, there is a very special place called "Fishtown." It is located where the river rushes over a picturesque dam and feeds into Lake Michigan. Situated on both banks are a number of unpainted, weather-beaten shanties, sheds and an ice house. It was once an active commercial fishing community. In the 1930s and '40s, there were eight family fishing operations working from those simple shacks. Nets were hung and dried in the sun, eight fishing tugs bounced beside the wharves, and the air was filled with the aroma of the hard wood that stoked smokehouses filled with chub, whitefish, and trout. Today the shanties house gift shops, boutiques, eateries, and a fleet of charter fishing boats. Only Carlson's remains an active fishery with two large smokers and three smaller ones. One tug and one trap netting boat operate from that location.

Because Fishtown is unique, it draws a multitude of those who love to shop, who like to eat, and, of course, fudgies. Mike Grosvenor recalls one who asked him, "Where can I catch smoked fish?"

In the old days, Fishtown was populated by a rich assortment of local characters. One of the most notable was Capt. George Cook. He was a commercial fisherman who worked the waters of Lake Michigan for at least fifty years. In his old age, he was a noted raconteur who spent summer days with his old buddies sitting on a bench outside the grocery store spinning yarns. When he gestured, one could see that he had only two fingers on one hand and a finger and a thumb on the other. He had lost four of them misusing an ice shaver and the other two to firecrackers. Nonetheless, he could make use of his remaining pinkies for such necessities as loading tobacco into his pipe. When Cook passed away at ninety-six, Bill Carlson said it was a good thing that he croaked before he ran out of fingers.

Capt. Cook had lived next door to the Carlsons. When Mark Carlson was a little boy, he had an experience with the captain that he'll never forget. The old man was seated in his back yard with a bucket in front of him, working with something that was white. Mark wondered aloud about it. "It's ice cream," stated Cook. "Do you want a taste?"

"You bet," said little Mark. Capt. Cook dipped in the bucket with a spoon and stuck it in the boy's mouth. Within seconds, Mark screamed and dashed for home and a spigot. What Capt. Cook had given him was not ice cream but a spoon full of freshly shaved horseradish.

Marvie Cook, the captain's son, was also a commercial fisherman and a Fishtown character. He worked on the family tug, in the fishery, and out on the docks doing chores. He most often dressed in rubber boots, gray shirt and pants, plus a flat, floppy hat with a short brim. When he mended nets on the dock, he looked the part of a seasoned seafarer, which he was. While performing the chore, he often drew the attention of fudgies with cameras. For them, it looked like a great northern Michigan photo opportunity. For Marvie, it was an irritation. So much so, that on certain days, when he was in a bad mood, he would work on the nets with his back toward the gathered tourists. Then he would carefully unbutton his trousers and let them slip slowly to his ankles. A slow, sly smile would cross his face as he heard ladies scream.

Unfortunately, two of Marvie's best friends were named Jack and Jim — Jack Daniels and Jim Beam. Those two pals of his led to many Fishtown tales. Like the time he was sitting on the dock in the late afternoon with the day's fishing done.

He was talking with his buddies while drinking what looked to be a Coke. However, as was his habit, he had dumped half the contents of the bottle and filled it back up with whiskey. He didn't want to be seen publicly imbibing. As he was talking, there was a loud "splat." A seagull in flight had just pooped and it hit right on the mouth of Marvie's bottle. He was in momentary shock. He shook his fist at the guilty bird and let out a stream of profanity. Calming down, he looked at his bottle, casually wiped off the top with his thumb, and took a big swig. Marvie was not known for wasting good whiskey.

While on the subject of booze, there are two accounts of what was called "The Fishtown Cocktail." The controversy swirls around an event that took place late each autumn, when all the tugs were pulled out of the river for repairs and winter storage. When the job was completed, it was time to celebrate. One of the fishermen was sent up to the Leland Mercantile to get a 2½-gallon pail, two quarts of vodka, and two bottles of Tom Collins mix. Those elements were swirled in the bucket and the party commenced. That's the recipe many remember and swear by. Others say that it was not necessary to have a celebration. A Fishtown Cocktail could be enjoyed at any time. The recipe for it was a glass, no ice, and bourbon. That was it.

A variation was the North Manitou Cocktail. It was composed of a glass, no ice, bourbon, and a sweet cherry. Which of these is the true version has been lost, as is the old name for Leland's river.

─

## Carp River Blues

A song by Jim Redmond
2003

Sittin' on the edge of that lazy Leland River.
Sittin' on the edge of that lazy Leland River.
I'm watchin' the boats go by,
And all I want to do is sit here.

Well, it's a lazy summer day in old Leland Town.
Well, it's a lazy summer day in old Leland Town.
I'm thinkin' 'bout swimmin',
Most likely I'll just lie down.

Days like today, slowly fade away.
Days like today, slowly fade away.
If I don't do nothin',
Well you know, that's okay.

"MOST OF THE TIME I DON'T DO ANYTHING...
AND I DON'T START THAT UNTIL ABOUT NOON." *

*A passing remark uttered by Leland's Jerry Muir

# Percy

Percy Guthrie was a thin man with a kindly grin. He wore spectacles, and one could tell that his thinning hair had once been red. He had been a commercial fisherman who worked for various Fishtown operations over the years. He was a committed bachelor who, as a younger man, still lived at home with his mother. He and his pal Marvie Cook spent time together at the bar in the Bluebird. A lot of time! So much so that the owners eventually put a metal plaque engraved with Percy's name on the back of his favorite bar chair. He was the only one in the Bluebird ever so honored.

His drinking irritated his mother to no end. So when Percy wove his way home after the bar closed at 2 a.m., she would regularly be waiting on the porch for him, standing in front of the door, blocking his entrance. Knowing that he had to be down on the fish tug in two hours, she would hand him his packed lunch bucket and send him to Fishtown. "Sleep on the boat," she would command. "That way you'll be there on time."

Then something happened that would change Percy's life. It was August 1941. At about 6 a.m. the Carlson's boat, *The Diamond,* which was out on Lake Michigan with Will Carlson and his son Pete aboard, had an engine explosion and the boat burned to the water line. The men had no radio to call for help. They were forced into Lake Michigan wearing cork life vests.

As the day wore on and darkness began to descend, folks in Fishtown became concerned. *The Diamond* should have returned hours before. The community's other fishermen climbed aboard their tugs and went out on the lake to look for their missing friends. It was a moonless night. They searched for hours with no sign of the Carlsons. Most of the boats returned to Leland shrouded in sadness. A few did not. Among them was a tug named *Irene* with Percy and Marvie aboard. To pass the time, they began to indulge in the whiskey they had brought aboard. They were looking for a needle in a haystack and the liquor was not helping them focus. However, at about 4 a.m., they came upon Pete who thrashed in the water to draw their attention. Percy and Marvie were wasted and had a terrible time trying to get him aboard. Finally, after countless failed attempts, they succeeded. Later they learned sadly that Will had not survived, but thankfully they had saved his son Pete.

It was an epiphany for Percy Guthrie. It haunted him that, because of the condition he was in, Pete

Carlson had almost been lost. The result was that he completely stopped drinking. As he grew older and commercial fishing became too strenuous for him, he took up house painting. He still frequented the Bluebird but drank no alcohol. He mellowed, except for times when he entered the bar to find some unknowing soul sitting in the chair where his name was inscribed. On those occasions, he would stand behind the stranger and glare until the trespasser, feeling uncomfortable, moved on.

In those later years, Percy became a beloved figure in Leland. He could often be found sitting on the bench beside the grocery store gabbing with old pals. As time passed, it became difficult for him to get around on foot. Sensing his dilemma, some of his buddies dreamed up a plan. It was early autumn and the formal golfing season was over, so it was possible to team up with the Leland Country Club to hold a tournament for his benefit, the Percy Guthrie Open. On the appointed day, golfers of all abilities — the good, the bad and the ugly — showed up. They paid their entrance fees and had a fabulous time. As the day drew to a close, they had raised enough money to present Percy with a brand-new golf cart to help him get around town. The Bluebird's Cris Telgard, one of the organizers, had gone to the sheriff beforehand to make sure that it would be okay for Percy to use the cart on the streets of the town. "Well," said the sheriff, "It's really not legal, but …." He then winked at Cris a couple of times. (Sheriffs giving winks in Leelanau County has been a tradition, as you'll discover in upcoming pages.)

Children, including my two daughters, Jennifer and Amy, loved to be around Percy and hear his stories. His influence was so profound that when my kids were given a kitty, they named it "Percy." However, as time went by, a problem arose. They discovered that their cat was a female! That, however, was not an issue for my kids. The name was not to be changed. They simply changed the spelling to "Purrrrcy."

# More miscellany

**Leelanau Enterprise** advertisement,
Dec. 25, 1930

CASH STORE PRICES

O.J. Plamondon

Lake Leelanau, Mich.

Sheepskin Coats .... $5.98

Men's Fleeced Union Suits .... 98 Cents

**Leelanau Enterprise** advertisement,
June 29, 1893

FRANK HAMILTON'S STORE

Suttons Bay, Mich.

Straws show which way the wind blows.

So will Straw Hats if they do not perfectly
fit the head.

It will hardly do for you to wear last year's
straw hat this season.

Our straw goods are now displayed in the
front part of our store ...

And we shall be pleased at any time to show
you the latest thing.

# The tip of the tip

## *A Little Town Called Northport*

By Larry Donovan McMachen
For the town's Sesquicentennial Celebration
1999

"If you've ever looked at Michigan, it's
    shaped much like a hand.
It's known throughout our nation as the
    'Water Wonderland.'
At the tip of the little finger is where this
    town began,
One hundred fifty years ago in northern
    Michigan."

(TO BE CONTINUED.)

It's fairly common for tourists from Indiana or
Illinois, heading for the Upper Peninsula, to mis-
takenly drive north up the Leelanau Peninsula.
They pull into Northport's gas station and ask,

"How much further to the bridge?" The answer is usually, "Unless your car is amphibious, go back the way you came."

～

Ray Kellogg has a story about the blacksmith in Northport. It begins in Kasson Township, where his great-grandfather settled and tried to farm in the 1890s. He had some Scottish heritage in him. He also had two sons, one of whom would become Ray's grandfather. The boys' favorite entertainment was going to a bar and starting a fight. There was a saying in the family that "an Irishman could get into a fight in an empty room. A Scotsman didn't need a room." That lifestyle wasn't very productive. Neither was the Kasson Township farm. Ray says that on that land, "You couldn't even raise hell with an axle jack or a fifth of whiskey." His future grandfather heard from some workers on a nearby railroad that Northport needed a blacksmith. They said, "There are seven blacksmiths in that town, but all of them are drunk. Nobody can get anything fixed or made in Northport."

Although Ray's grandfather wasn't a trained blacksmith, he was good with his hands and knew a bit about working with iron and steel. So, he decided to give it a try. He told the family, "If there's anything there for me, I'll call for you. If not, I'll come back home." In short order, he was the only blacksmith in town and moved the family to Northport. That was in the early part of the 20<sup>th</sup> century.

He built a house in town with pens in back to hold all kinds of livestock. That's because many of his clients paid in barter. Ray's grandfather was not very outgoing. Therefore, the "good old boys" hung out at the carpenter's shop in town where there was laughter and practical joking. Within their group was a very gullible guy who could be counted on to carry out silly tasks. One day, they sent him to the blacksmith's shop to bring back "a hundred yards of shore line." Another time, he was directed to go there and buy a "a round square-punch." Ray's grandfather got the last laugh on that one. He sent back a piece of iron that was square on one end and round on the other, along with a bill for five dollars — a pretty penny in those days.

If Ray's grandfather was dour, he combined it with a reputation for little patience. One day, a man came in with a highly spirited horse needing a single shoe. Grandpa was busy, but since it was just one horseshoe, he took on the job. He had the horse's back hoof between his knees when the animal delivered a ferocious kick. Grandpa flew up in the air, breaking a sky light. He dusted himself off (Ray swears this is true), walked around to the front of the horse, and delivered a fearsome knockout punch. He then replaced the shoe on the motionless steed.

> MORAL: NEXT TIME YOU GO TO YOUR NEIGHBORHOOD BLACKSMITH'S SHOP, DON'T HORSE AROUND.

‿

To the east of Northport, in Grand Traverse Bay, there is a tiny piece of land. It was originally named Bellows Island, but because it is a traditional nesting place for cormorants and gulls (thousands of them), everyone in Northport calls it Gull Island. Around 1910, a misguided individual built a rather large cottage there, but only occupied it for one summer. The birds drove him out. Over the years the building was vandalized and fell into ruin. Only two tall stone chimneys remain standing. Often fudgies, seeing that curious sight out in the bay, ask a local about it. They sometimes get the answer, "Oh, that's a grounded submarine. It was sent here to guard against any Canadian invasion."

‿

Underwater craft seem to play an important part

in Northport's lore. Sometimes a young swain will ask a pretty girl if she'd like to see the submarine races. If the answer is in the affirmative, the couple drives at sunset to the nearby Lake Michigan beach called Peterson Park.

BOY: "Watch closely. The submarines only surface for a second or two. (Pause) Oh, there was one. Did you see it?"

GIRL: "No."

BOY: "I think you might be sitting at the wrong angle. Come over here closer to me. There, that's good. Keep looking."

I think you get the picture.

‿

"If you've ever been to Northport, then
    you'll know just what I mean,
The people in this little town are living
    out a dream.
A dream that all Americans have had
    a time or two,
A little town, a little church and
    a little country school."

(TO BE CONTINUED)

‿

Ray Kellogg remembers a story about one of Northport's classic characters. He was a rotund guy named Pete who usually had a cigar sticking out of his mouth. Stuff just seemed to happen to him. He worked at the town's canning factory, which was located on the bay. It was early summer, and the boss wanted to get the place in shipshape condition for the coming cherry harvest. There was a very large pipe on the side of the building that functioned mostly as a drain, dumping water that had washed the cherries. Pete and two migrant workers, neither of whom spoke English, were assigned to clean out the pipe, removing critters, leaves, and accumulated sand. The migrants worked on its upper level, Pete at the pipe's lower end. He was using a shovel to clear the opening. Things were going well enough for him until his shovel got stuck in the pipe. Pete waved and called for the migrants to come help him. Because they understood no English, they determined that Pete was asking them to turn on the water. Pete was peering in closely at his shovel as a great torrent blasted from the pipe. The migrants were astonished by the sight of Pete flying into the bay, followed by a line of blue cigar smoke.

᷍

Kathy Firestone recalls an episode demonstrating how easy life can be in Leelanau County. It is about one of Northport's favorite characters, Bill Livingston. He was an intellectual who had earned a degree in botany from the University of Wisconsin. He discovered, however, that the academic life was not his calling. He preferred to work with his hands. He brought his family north in the 1950s and began building wooden sailboats in a long shed near Northport's marina. As it turned out, his masterfully built boats were highly prized. He was also a gifted conversationalist and the self-appointed town philosopher. Summer and winter, he worked in his shop bare-footed. One day in the early '60s, a visitor found her way to his workshop. Bill welcomed her and a long conversation ensued as he continued to work. After returning to her downstate home, the visitor wanted to send Bill a thank-you note but could not remember his name. So, she simply addressed the envelope: "To the barefoot boat builder, Northport, MI." No problem. Bill Livingston received the letter.

&#x202f;

"Through my life, I've traveled far and wide,
But I envy those in Northport,
who have lived there all their lives."

# Miscellany again

**Leelanau Enterprise**, November 1895

"George Gagnon of Northport says he thinks the government owes him a pension as now he has 47 grandchildren and 24 of his own."

◡

**Leelanau Enterprise**, July 1920

"Oliver Brow of Provemont has brought his restaurant right up to date with the installation of a telephone."

◡

**Leelanau Enterprise**, Aug. 31, 1944

"George Howard has a victory garden this year, measuring 10 feet by 10 feet. In the spring, he bought $5 worth of wire to fence it in. To date he has had 4 cucumbers and 2 tomatoes."

# Animal crackers

Dave Ball, the highly respected builder and restorer of wooden boats, lives near Maple City. At one time, he had a well-used Pinto car that he really loved. Because it was old, he didn't garage it, regularly parking it just outside his home beside a large, beautiful pine tree. One morning he tried to start his Pinto and couldn't. It was dead. He inspected the car and discovered that a porcupine had eaten all the belts, hoses and brake linings! Oooohh, that really made him mad. He happened to look up and there in his beautiful pine tree was the guilty porcupine. Dave ran into the house and grabbed a pistol. He fired at the critter, emptying the gun. Either he missed six times, or the quills deflected the bullets. It didn't really matter to the porcupine. It simply moved methodically higher and higher up the tree. But it mattered to Dave. Again, he flew into the house and this time, using instinctive Leelanau County creativity, grabbed an axe, chopped down his pine tree, and dispatched the varmint with the implement at hand.

MORAL: IF AT FIRST YOU DON'T SUCCEED,
MAKE A NEW PLAN AND "HATCH-ET."

~

**Leelanau Enterprise**, Jan. 4, 1945

"The farmers around Port Oneida are most grateful to 12-year-old Eddie Klett who is the prize fox trapper in the neighborhood. To date, Eddie has caught four foxes, thus saving the neck of many a Port Oneida chicken."

~

For years, Mike Grosvenor, of the Manitou Island Transit, ferried people from Leland to the Manitou Islands. To satisfy hunger and thirst, he sold soft drinks and snacks aboard his boat, the *Mishe-Mokwa*. Mike would safely secure the munchies overnight as best he could. But during one summer, he began to notice that some of the snacks, particularly potato chips, were missing in the mornings. It was a mystery until one day he noticed an unusual odor in the pilot house. He looked around and discovered a raccoon asleep in a cubbyhole. It wasn't bothering anybody, so Mike ignored it for the time being. He was pleased that he had solved the problem of the missing potato chips. He headed off for South Manitou with a boat full of campers and tourists.

Once back in port in Leland, there was a crew change and the job of cleaning up the boat for the evening cocktail cruise. Mike, who is known for having an unusual sense of humor, sent a young female employee up to the pilot house telling her to mop well, including every nook and cranny. A crowd was gathering on the dock, anticipating a relaxing ride on Lake Michigan. Suddenly they heard a bloodcurdling scream. Crew members rushed to the pilot house where a grand commotion was under way with lots of yelling, topped by the girl's high-pitched screams. Seventy-five people watched in awe from the dock as crew members flew about the pilot house swinging mops and brooms. Finally, the fat raccoon, in a nasty mood, jumped to the dock and waddled through the startled crowd. Mike smiled with satisfaction. "We scared that raccoon so bad he'll never be back," he told the crew with conviction. The next morning when Mike boarded the *Mishe-Mokwa*, he noticed that the potato chips were missing.

ب

Mark Carlson bought an older home in Leland that he knew needed some fixing up. What he wasn't prepared for was the discovery of a skunk living under it. So, Mark got hold of Old Joe Schwartz, who had the reputation as the best varmint catcher in Leelanau County. Mark watched with awe as Old Joe prepared for the task. He went to the Leland Mercantile and procured some discarded chicken skins. He skillfully baited a livetrap and carefully set it in just the right place. The next morning Mark arose with great anticipation. He was thrilled to see that the trap had sprung. He approached it warily only to discover he had caught his best friend Malcolm Chatfield's cat.

⌣

Scott Anderson and his pal Jim were at the Bluebird one evening shooting pool and drinking beer. As the bar was closing, they decided to go to Scott's house for one more. On the way, they saw a skunk that had been run over and killed. In addition, they discovered two tiny skunk kits. Being kindhearted guys, they picked them up and carried them to Scott's house. Within a short time, a question arose, "What do we do with them now?" Scott came up with the solution. He remembered a neighbor who loved animals. Scott has often wondered what the neighbor thought the next morning when he opened his garage door to find two skunk kits and a can of cat food.

～

Bill and Barb Klein bought a floral business in Suttons Bay and moved there in 1965. They would become an admired and beloved couple in the community. As new arrivals, however, they knew nary a soul. In his second week in town, Bill took a walk in the business district to get a feel for the village. With him was his beagle, Herman. Unfortunately, the dog saw something of interest and took off after it. Bill began shouting at the top of his lungs, "Herman, you bad boy! Stop! Herman! You get right back here! Now!!!" He couldn't understand why so many people on the street turned to look at him with alarmed expressions. In time, he would learn that many men in Suttons Bay had first names of Herman. As a last name, it was even more common. There was a Herman Service Station, a Herman Excavating Company, and a Herman Road, named for the large local family. It got worse. One evening, Bill decided to attend a Village Council meeting, just to get acquainted. About 15 minutes into the agenda, the phone rang. It was answered by one of the officials who then asked, "Is there a Bill Klein here?" Bill made his presence known. "Well," said the official, "You're needed at home. Someone there named Herman just got skunked."

~

**Leelanau Enterprise**, April 28, 1945

From the editor

"Last Friday, when I went down to the Glen Lake Narrows, I saw Elmer Billman driving across the bridge. Running alongside the car was a dog, a bird dog, I think. The picture reminded me of trackmen or boxers in training, running to keep themselves in trim, so I thought Elmer must be putting his dog through his paces. Maybe it was a new angle on getting a bird. As Elmer made the turn at the corner, I asked him if he was training his dog? 'No,' he said. 'I'm punishing him.' I wonder if he learned his lesson?"

**Leelanau Enterprise**, July 14, 1945

"In order that his dog will not miss any of the excitement, Mr. Alphonse LaBonte, of Lake Leelanau, has built a platform complete with a parasol to keep off the hot sun or driving rain. The platform is approached by steps which the dog mounts with much grace and dignity. From his private throne, he can watch the comings and goings between the village and points east."

**Leelanau Enterprise**, March 1894

"At a party on North Manitou Island on Christmas, one of the persons in attendance killed Capt. Oleson's dog. The killer had sandy hair and has not been apprehended."

**Leelanau Enterprise**, December 1885

"A few short-sighted citizens of Leland still permit their hogs to run wild in the streets of our beautiful village. The unsightliness of such a practice is bad enough, but the after effects are much worse."

**Leelanau Enterprise**, Sept. 10, 1896

"Jake says that if one of his neighbors had not tied tin pans, pails and washtubs to his cow's tail she would not have been sick, but as it is, he has very little hopes for her recovery."

## Leelanau Enterprise, May 17, 1945

From the editor

"I feel very guilty in not having sent some suggestions to Nan Helm on the big problem of naming her new cow. [Nan had written to the *Enterprise* earlier with her dilemma and suggesting she might name it Sweet Face.] But *Enterprise* reader Dale Reynolds objected to Sweet Face and said that Nan's cow should have a name more in keeping with the beautiful Glen Lake region where she will make her home. So, here's what I suggest, Nan. Why not call her 'Belle'? The word means 'beautiful' in French. You could elaborate on it, if you wish, making it 'Isabella,' 'Lulu Belle,' or even 'La Belle, the beautiful.'"

I heard the following story so many times, it must be true. A woman living along M22 north of Glen Arbor called the sheriff's office complaining about the number of deer being killed on the road near her home. "It seems to be happening close to the sign that reads 'Deer Crossing,'" she said. "Could you move the sign to another place that might be safer for them?"

**Leelanau Enterprise**, May 31, 1945

From Homer B. Fouts of Omena

"We feel compelled to take issue with the editor to hang a Belle on Nan Helm's cow. A cowbell is associated with such boisterous affairs as shivarees and a bell-cow is never found leading the cloistered life we predict for Sweet Face."

Bill Carlson has many talents. For a period of time, he was a guide for deer hunters. He tells the story of being on a hunt on North Manitou Island with a Native American man named Archie Miller. To this day, Bill credits Miller with being the greatest guide he has ever known. On this day, Bill and Archie had a single client. As they moved carefully through the forest, they sighted a beautiful buck. Archie motioned for his client to fire. He did — and missed. The deer stood frozen. The client fired again — and missed again. Then a third time with the same result. Archie grabbed his rifle, growling, "You can't scare 'em to death," and brought down the buck.

**Leelanau Enterprise**, June 14, 1945

Attention Nan Helm

"Mrs. Lottie Kelderhouse of Port Oneida sends the following names for your cow: Daisydean, Violet and Snowball."

Phil Deering grew up on a farm that abutted the village of Empire. The Deerings were the long-time, highly regarded owners of the town's grocery store. Unfortunately, Phil's father also raised horses. I say "unfortunately" because he was notorious for not keeping his fences in good repair. As a result, the horses were always getting loose and roaming the village and surrounding farms. One horse named "Billy" was particularly rambunctious and had to be watched carefully. Even when fenced in, he could find a weak spot. One day, Billy got loose and went into the village where he climbed up on a woman's porch and began nuzzling the door knob, apparently trying to get in. The woman came out of the house screaming. She aimed a mighty kick at Billy, missed, and broke her ankle. Of course, Phil's father paid the bill, saying, "You know, I've got to fix those fences."

The next disaster happened in the churchyard, where the sexton had dug a grave for tomorrow's burial. He had carefully covered the open grave with plywood. It was early November, and that night there was a dusting of snow. Also that night, the Deering horses got loose. One named "Penny" grazed her way into the churchyard. The snow camouflaged the plywood. Penny stepped on it, it gave way, and she went feet first into the grave. The good news was that Penny wasn't hurt. The bad news was that she couldn't get out. As daylight arrived, passing motorists were shocked to see a horse's head sticking out of an open grave! The bread delivery man came into the grocery store laughing and said to Phil's father, "Darndest thing I ever saw. There's a live horse in a grave over at the churchyard!" His dad put two and two together quickly. Phil got the phone call. Because he was the oldest child, he was told to get Penny out of the hole. Phil sat down and tried to figure out how to solve the problem. Meanwhile, folks kept coming into the store saying, "You won't believe this. There's a horse over there in a grave!" Phil got a shovel and started digging at one end of the hole to make a ramp. With lots of sweat and thrown dirt, Phil got Penny out. The sexton was forced to dig the grave again and Phil's father had to pay the church one hundred dollars for the extra work. He was heard to say, "You know, I've got to fix those fences."

Years later, Phil was dating a girl named Sue who had summered in Empire. In fact, the courting had gone so well that they decided to get married. One day, he happened to tell her the story about the horse falling into the grave. Sue stopped him saying, "I've heard that story before." "You have?" replied Phil. "Yes," she answered. "That was my grandfather's grave." That revelation did not turn out to have grave consequences. They got married anyway.

MORAL: DESPITE THE POPULAR ADAGE, ONCE IN A WHILE WHEN YOU'RE IN A HOLE, IT'S JUST BETTER TO KEEP ON DIGGING.

‿

**Leelanau Enterprise**, Aug. 2, 1945

"Shame on Dale Reynolds of Empire for not suggesting a name for Nan Helm's cow. He started the whole thing, you remember, by not approving of Nan's name of 'Sweet Face' for her bovine."

‿

The following animal story inspired the subtitle for this book. Bill Carlson, his wife Jennifer, and their son Asher were hunting deer. Jennifer was secured in a blind, high in a tree. Bill and Asher were in another part of the woods. Bill got a text from his wife, saying that she might be in trouble. There was a bear lolling on the ground directly below her. Bill told her to stay calm; he and Asher would get there as soon as possible. They moved carefully through the underbrush until they drew near to Jennifer's tree. There, indeed, was a black bear. A big one! Bill kept edging closer and closer to it. Asher whispered, "Dad, he's awfully near! Aren't you scared?" "No," Bill also whispered. "Look at your feet. You have on big boots. I'm wearing tennis shoes. All I have to do is outrun you."

~

Intensive research into the late summer and early fall issues of the 1945 *Leelanau Enterprise* yielded no further mentions of Nan Helm's cow. Sadly, what she was finally named is lost to history.

"IT'S A POKE AND PLUM TOWN."

QUESTION: WHAT DID THE PRETTY
BLOND SAY WHEN SHE SAW A BEACH
FULL OF HANDSOME YOUNG GUYS?

ANSWER: "OH! MEN!! AHHH!!!"

## Ode to Omena

By Larry McMachen
2002

There's a town in northern Michigan,
Omena is the name.
It's a town with lots of history,
But not a lot of fame.
Now the people in this little town
They're few and far between.
Their weekly coffee hour
Is the most important thing.

When I was a boy
Growing up in that town,
We used to call Omena
The poke and plum town.
We had that little nickname
When we would joke around.
You'd poke your head out the window
And you were plum out of town.

‿

Writer Amanda Holmes remembers a long-term resident saying, "Omena has only one corner and no one stops for that." As you drive into Omena from the north, that corner is prominent. It is a sharp curve to the right, barely skirting Grand Traverse Bay. If those new to the area miscalculate, they drive into the drink. It occurs often enough that folks in Northport have dubbed it "The Omena Car Wash."

~

**Leelanau Enterprise**, April 8, 1897

"Johnnie of Omena will not be sailing this summer. It is reported that he has closer attractions near home."

~

During the summer in the late '60s and early '70s the Omena Bar was a very popular place on Friday nights when they featured an "All You Can Eat Fried Fish Dinner." Of course, with the coming of September and the start of school, tourists would leave and the bar business would fall off markedly. So, one year, the owners decided to add a special autumn event, a weekly "All You Can Eat Steak Night." That news was of special interest to two citizens of the village of Lake Leelanau — Bruce Price, a mason and strawberry farmer, and Emil Bunek, a plumber. Both were large men with reputations as renowned trenchermen. They arrived together on the evening of the steak deal debut at the Omena Bar. To the astonishment of the assembled diners and the shock of the management, they downed four steaks each. The result was that the opening night of "All You Can Eat Steak Night" was also its closing night.

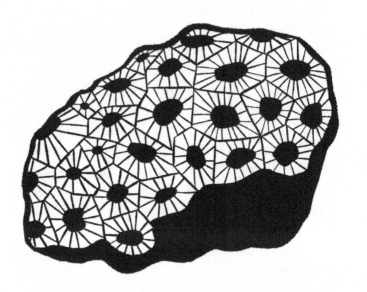

# The Petoskey

Petoskey stones are composed of a fossilized freshwater coral that lived some four hundred million years ago. When the stone is dry it looks like limestone, but when it's wet it shows off a distinctive pentagonal pattern. When polished, it can be made into beautiful jewelry. In 1967 it was designated the state stone of Michigan. Leelanau County is blessed with a profusion of them, but it takes a practiced eye to find one.

Kevin Gauthier is a confessed rock hound. He owns the Korner Gem in Greilickville, which features cases full of beautiful jewelry designed around stunning polished stones. There are rings, pendants, necklaces, bracelets, belt buckles and more. The rocks come from all over the country, but the shop specializes in Michigan stones and the star in Kevin's show is the Michigan Petoskey stone. One of his greatest pleasures is going out to find them. One afternoon, while searching on a Leelanau County beach, he noticed a father and small son looking for Petoskeys as well. He could see they weren't having any luck, so Kevin moved ahead of them and planted a beauty where they would be sure to find it. Then he slid up into the beach grass and sat down to watch. It was the boy who made the discovery. "Look, Dad," he shouted. "I found a real Petoskey!" He showed it proudly to his father, and then to Kevin's horror, the kid skipped it into Lake Michigan.

ৎ

Bill Chatfield was well known in Leland as a rascal. He could find humor in almost anything. In the 1970s the Leelanau County Sheriff decided it was necessary to raise money to buy a drug-sniffing dog. They held a public gathering to present the idea. There was some lively discussion, but Bill Chatfield capped the evening when he rose and said, "I don't think we need a drug-sniffing dog. I believe we'd be a lot better off getting a dog that can find Petoskey stones."

# Miscellany once more

**Leelanau Enterprise**, March 23, 1920

"We have been informed that many Leland citizens now in Florida are ill with flu.

MORAL: Spend your winters in Leland and stay well."

~

A woman walked into Leelanau Books and said she was just browsing, simply looking for something good to read. The clerk suggested a trilogy he had just finished. "Oh, I love trilogies," the woman stated. "I just finished one. It had seven parts."

~

Rich Bahle remembers a time when the family store in Suttons Bay sold cloth cut from bolts. One day a woman came in, made a selection and had the clerk, Lois Bahle, cut her a specific length. Several days later the woman came back saying, "I've decided I don't like the pattern on this cloth, and I want to return it." Lois replied, "I'm afraid I can't do that. It was cut to your specified length." The lady began to fume, finally huffing, "I want to talk to your father about this." Lois said her father was at lunch and would return shortly. "I'll wait right here for him," she sniffed. When Owen Bahle arrived, the woman marched up to him and sternly asked, "May I return this cloth?" "Sure," answered Owen. He put the cloth under his arm, strode to his office, and didn't come back.

**Leelanau Enterprise**, Feb. 23, 1893

"Ye Editor has gone to Detroit and the *Enterprise* is in charge of the devil and the quad splitter* this week."

*Note: A quad splitter was an apprentice in a newspaper shop who performed a number of simple tasks.. He was not a writer. Therefore, we must assume that the next edition of the *Enterprise* was written and edited by Lucifer.

## A Song of Glen Lake

Words and Music by Nancy Helm
1943

Green are your hills, blue are your skies
Like India's jewels, your waters lie.
Your glorious sunsets, filled with rainbow
    gleams
Glen Lake, the lovely lake, of you I dream.
O thou lovely lake,
Lake so wondrous and fair.
I hear you calling,
Calling me there.
Where your sun kissed beaches lie,
Under a blue, blue sky.
Glen Lake — the lovely lake,
A bit of Paradise.

(Note: Ms. Helm could not come up with a name
    for her cow, but she could write song lyrics.)

# The runaway

Little four-year-old Amy came out of her Leland cottage and let the screen door slam behind her. She was carrying her teddy bear and a tiny suitcase meant for doll clothes. There was a frown on her face. Her father was working in the yard. "What's up?" he asked. "I'm wunning away," she stated with authority. "You want to talk about it?" "No," she answered firmly. "OK," her father said. "You can run away. Just don't cross the street." "All wight," said a miffed Amy. She walked up to the corner and sat down in the shade of a leafy maple tree. As he worked, her father glanced in her direction occasionally. Sometimes she was talking to Teddy. Other times she just sat silently. In the late afternoon, her mother started to roast a chicken. The kitchen windows were open, and a delicious aroma spread across the neighborhood. Amy rose, picked up Teddy and the suitcase, and skipped just a bit as she returned. The frown was gone when she entered the cottage.

MORAL: IT'S OK TO WUN AWAY AS LONG AS YOU DON'T CROSS THE STREET AND ARE BACK HOME IN TIME FOR SUPPER.

# John Barleycorn

**Leelanau Enterprise**, April 25, 1893

"It is said that Wm. Mosier has rented his saloon to Daniel Sieber, who will run it as a temperance resort."

There was once a hotel in Northport on the main street. The ground floor of the building housed a tavern. A neon sign on the side of the structure read:

"Hotel
Liquor"

As years went by, residents forgot the actual name of the place and just called it the "Hotel Liquor."

"The Floating Palace Saloon, which has been docked at the pier in Northport, left the village for a stay at another port. On the Sunday following the departure, the ministers of Northport held a temperance meeting at the Methodist church in which they worked themselves to a frenzied pitch over the evils of intemperance, but all residents of Northport are in full belief that the beautiful village, Northport, is still a moral and virtuous town, the ministers to the contrary."

Art's Tavern in Glen Arbor first opened its doors in 1926. It's legendary for good food and drink. Tim Barr, who has owned the establishment since 2000, reports that during the summer months he serves 175 pounds of hamburger a day. It is an inviting, family-friendly place where there is almost never trouble. Almost. Tim remembers when a long-time friend from downstate came into Arts. He was a member of the State Police bomb squad, in his career he had seen a lot. Tim sat down with him, and his friend told him he had come north to relax. Tim replied, "This is a good place to start. There are never any problems here." Just then a fight broke out between two women. When Tim rushed over to stop it, one of the women hit him with her flip-flop. The bartender entered the fray, grabbing the other woman. As she squirmed to get loose, her tank top slipped off. She dove under a table. Fight over. Peace returned to Art's.

Another of those rare brawls occurred some years earlier. In that case, Tim says God intervened. It was a summer night like any other. However, a small tussle erupted into a major battle. Tables were overturned. Glasses were broken. Tim was at a loss. He, the bartender and the waiters entered the fight, pushing the rowdies into the street where the melee got even worse. That's when the miracle happened. A bolt of lightning hit an electrical transformer on a pole across the street. Sparks and shrapnel flew in all directions. All the lights in town went out. Huge drops of rain drenched the brawlers. Everyone ran for cover. To this day, Tim believes it was divine intervention that ended the fight.

Dick's Pour House in Lake Leelanau is another of the county's iconic watering holes. It is everything a country tavern should be. There are mounted deer heads and humongous stuffed fish on every wall. Dick's serves great hearty meals and has a welcoming bar. It is also peacefully family-friendly. Usually. There was a time, however, when Bruce Price and Emil Bunek (the same guys who closed down Steak Night at the Omena Bar) got into a row. Both were very big men and as their squabble turned into an altercation, the two men went flying through the door and out on the sidewalk. In so doing, they took out the door frame. The next morning, bright and early, they both returned in pickup trucks carrying lumber and tools, and together they rebuilt the door. Such is life in a small town.

**Leelanau Enterprise**, February 1895

"Leland saloons and hotels reaped quite a harvest last week during court week. It was very fortunate for the saloon keepers that the weather was decidedly warmer than it was the previous week, as during the severe cold of the week before, all whiskeys froze and the bums around Leland will long remember they were forced to go sober."

# The poet

Author Aaron Stander tells a story about a young couple who, on their first date, went to the Bluebird in Leland. The young man could only afford dinner in the bar room. (The happy ending to the story is that the couple did end up getting married.) On this evening, they had just ordered dinner when an unusual-looking man entered. He had a mop of unruly hair, wore a dirty T-shirt with a hole in it, and his pants looked like they hadn't seen a washing machine for a while. He moved directly behind the bar, poured himself a glass of bourbon (no ice), and looked around the room. In a gravelly voice he bellowed, "Where's all the pu..y?" The startled young couple called the waiter over and asked, "Who is that guy?" "Oh," replied the waiter, "that's the world-famous poet, Jim Harrison."

Jim Harrison was one of our country's finest writers. We were lucky to have had him among us in Leelanau County for some 30 years. He was a prolific author whose work includes 14 books of poetry, 12 novels, 10 collections of novellas, and numerous works of nonfiction. At least three of his works were made into motion pictures, the most famous being "Legends of the Fall." Jim was also famous for his love of food and drink. He especially enjoyed copious amounts of red wine. He and his wife Linda were marvelous chefs whose dinners were works of art, often taking days of preparation. I remember sitting in his backyard having a drink on a Tuesday afternoon and watching Jim and a friend kill a goose and bury it, the start of Sunday's cassoulet. He was a dinner guest at our home on numerous occasions and was always a great raconteur.

Jim was, by his own admission, a gourmand. He was known for sometimes ordering two or three entrees at a single meal. He told the story of having a lunch with Orson Welles at one the actor's favorite Los Angeles restaurants. As I remember, they had several cocktails, multiple appetizers, and a couple of entrees each. Of course, wine flowed throughout. The meal ended with an array of desserts, coffee, brandy and cigars. As the two left the restaurant, Jim was stunned to see Welles talking to the maître d', making reservations for dinner that night.

A wise man once advised me, "Work hard and play hard — and know the difference between the two." I believe Jim personified that adage. In public, he could be funny, outrageous and sometimes crude. For those who didn't know him, that could be problematic. What they didn't understand was that, in addition to being a genius, he was a dedicated, disciplined writer who worked diligently every day. In order to do that, he demanded privacy at home. A sign at the entrance of his driveway read, "Do not come in if you have not phoned first. This means you."

Jim once told his friend Norm Wheeler, "When I first moved here and was a struggling writer, people said I was a drunk. Now that I've had some best sellers and a hit movie, they say I'm a 'problem drinker.'"

Wayne Wunderlich lives on the outskirts of the village of Lake Leelanau near the Harrison farm. Wayne remembers a time when a young writer friend from out of town came for a visit. "I understand the famous Jim Harrison lives up here," he said. "I want to meet him." "Oh," replied Wayne, "he lives here all right but don't go to his house. That would be an awful mistake. If you want to see him, go to Dick's Pour House tomorrow at about 5:30 and sit at the bar. A guy will likely come in whose clothes will have a few holes in them. His hair will be messed up and one of his eyes wanders. In other words, he'll look fearsome. That's Harrison. Do not talk to him unless he talks to you. Got it?" His friend left for Dick's and vowed to behave as instructed. When he returned, Wayne asked how it went. "Fine," he replied proudly. "Harrison came in just as you said he would. After about half an hour, he asked me a question, and from then on we had a good time." "Great," replied Wayne. "Don't try it again."

Dennis Gripentrog, of Maple City, remembers Jim telling a story about a book signing. A woman came up to him, much in awe of being in the presence of the great writer. "Oh, Mr. Harrison," she gasped. "I'm interested in your reputation as a fine gourmet. I'm curious. What do you like to eat for breakfast?" Jim replied, "I usually start with a platter of warmed-over cheerleaders."

As many of you know, a magnum of wine is a large bottle. It contains the equivalent of two standard bottles of wine. Jim once commented to Norm Wheeler, "They should stop making magnums of wine. A magnum is a worthless size. It's too much for lunch and not enough for dinner."

Harrison had a voluminous vocabulary. Readers of his writings recognized that, but so did those who spent time with him on a regular basis. Scott Anderson worked at his family's appliance store where Harrison was a customer. He got a phone call one night about ten o'clock from Jim. "Scotty," he said. "My refrigerator is making ghastly noises!" Anderson wasn't sure how to respond, but came up with, "Since the noises are just 'ghastly,' I'll be over in the morning."

When Geno Miller was a young man, he was walking across the parking lot of the Bluebird when he saw Jim, who said, "I understand you are going to take an extended trip to France." "That's right." replied Geno. "Let me give you some advice," Harrison continued. "Treat the French women with great contempt. They love that from Americans. Do that, and you'll score big time. I know. I've been there many times." When Geno returned, he again ran into Jim, who asked, "Well?" Geno answered, "I never got close enough to a French woman to treat her with even the slightest bit of contempt." Jim replied in his patented growl, "I'm very disappointed in you."

# Miscellany also

**Leelanau Enterprise**. Dec. 26, 1895

"George Biglow and Phillip Howell of Northport were here on Tuesday. Phillip secured his marriage license. Consequently, a big smile illuminated his countenance."

⌣

**Leelanau Enterprise**, Nov. 20, 1930

"Si Timblepaugh says he can read his wife like a book, but he can't shut her up like one."

⌣

**Leelanau Enterprise**, Dec. 16, 1897

"County Clerk Hinshaw says he has eleven divorce cases on the docket for trial next term of court and that marriage is a failure to some people in the county."

GETTING THE MORNING
MAIL IN SUTTONS BAY.

# By the bay

Rich Bahle remembers that when he was growing up in Suttons Bay, the cuisine in the kitchens of the town was not terribly exciting. "A pot roast," he says, "was considered gourmet food, especially if it was accompanied by potatoes with chopped parsley on them."

～

His sister Lois says that well into the '60s, there were only two sheriff's squad cars in Leelanau County. Everyone in Suttons Bay knew the exact time of the afternoon crew shift. That's when both cruisers would be at the courthouse in Leland. It was at that exact time that folks in Suttons Bay put their boats in the water in spring and pulled them out in the fall. Why buy a license plate for your boat trailer when you only needed it two days a year?

～

There was once a train that ran through the village of Suttons Bay. Its route went from Traverse City to Northport. No one seems to remember the real name of the railroad because everyone in town called it the B.& F. E., which stood for "Back and Forth Empty."

⟶

From 1938 into the mid '80s, the county Rotary Club met in the Grange Hall in Suttons Bay. It is a tidy, narrow, one-story white building a block off the main drag. The club had no trouble getting members, for one good reason: The food! Behind the meeting room stood a simple kitchen with one electric range and two wood stoves. That cook-house was staffed by a half-dozen elderly ladies. It was said that the youngest was 85. Those women were steadfastly loyal to their job of feeding the Rotarians once a week at noon. They were also magicians of the galley. Their baked chicken was fabulous. Nobody made better dinner rolls. Their mashed potatoes and gravy were known county-wide. And their vegetables were perfect. I was lucky enough to have lunch there once and, as a side dish, they served fresh creamed peas with tiny little potatoes. The last time I ate that delectable combination was at my great-grandmother's farm.

Yet the *pièce de résistance* was the pie. From those simple wood stoves came meringue pies, cream pies, apple, peach, raisin and, of course, cherry pies. Each was better than the other. It's said that folks almost came to fisticuffs just to join Rotary for the remarkable down-home cuisine. After the meetings, the women cleaned up and played euchre. It's said that on one occasion, a cook well into her 90s, was hospitalized in Traverse City. At five in the morning, on meeting day, she rose from her hospital bed and demanded to be driven to the Suttons Bay Grange Hall. She could not be dissuaded. No ifs, ands, or buts. Rotary was meeting and she was needed. She performed her culinary duties and went back to the hospital. No one remembers whether she paused to play euchre before returning.

# Earl the pearl

In, Suttons Bay, a town known for its share of nonconformists, Earl Chervenka stands out. He had a sturdy build, wore badly smudged glasses, and an old hat covered with a wide assortment of badges — some of which were in very poor taste. His wardrobe was a study in mismatches. He had been a Seabee who served in Italy during WWII. According to Larry Mawby he was a remarkably talented guy without a formal education and not much respect for those who did.

His place of business, the Rung and Bung Works, was housed in what was once the town's livery stable. To say that Earl was a jack of all trades is an understatement. He fixed stuff, mended stuff and created stuff. For example, he produced paddle boards before anybody knew how to use them. He could weld. He made signs. He was even a taxidermist. His slogan emblazoned on the wall was, "If it has fins, feathers, or fur, I'll mount it for you."

The interior of his shop was a world-class mess. The floor was always about eight inches deep in sawdust and wood chips. There was a variety of tools, paints, glues, chemicals and half-finished projects. He used to say, "If I can't fix it for you or make it for you, you don't need it."

Earl obtained a flatbed truck and on it he cobbled together an ingenious crane. It looked outlandish but it worked. He used it to lower boats into the bay in the spring and hoist them out in the fall. He accomplished these jobs with help from his brother, Ron. As they worked, Earl and Ron shouted orders at each other — orders that often conflicted. That's when, at the top of their lungs, they displayed a remarkable and creative talent for profanity. Folks in Suttons Bay remember the air actually turning blue. That's how Chervenka earned the title "Earl the Pearl."

Will Case-Daniels told me that Earl did not like his judgement to be challenged. He remembered that a woman came into the Rung and Bung Works carrying a wooden wagon wheel. She asked Earl if he could turn it into a chandelier. He assured her that he could accomplish it with ease and told her to come back in a week. When she returned, she was pleased with Earl's creation. "How much do I owe you?" she asked. "Two hundred fifty dollars," Earl replied. The woman was shocked. "That's too much," she sniffed. "I'll not pay more than one hundred fifty dollars." Earl happened to be standing next to his band saw. He grabbed the wagon wheel chandelier and cut it into nine pieces. He put them in a box, handed it to her and pointed to the door. Earl didn't fool around.

Rich Bahle recalls a time, soon after the Environmental Protection Act was passed. Somehow, the EPA got wind of the Rung and Bung Works and sent an inspector to Suttons Bay to check it out. Once there, he handed Earl a pen and a clipboard with a piece of paper on it. "Take a look at that," said the inspector, "and check off any of those items you have and how much and how many." Earl eyed the inspector suspiciously but did as instructed and passed it back. "Oh my! Oh my!!" said the EPA man. "You need to have a license for this and for that and permits for these and for those. And of course, there will be all kinds of fees to pay." "Give that clipboard back," ordered Earl. He took the pen and began saying things like, "I used that up. I made a mistake on that one. I never had this one either." By the time he was done, he had crossed out everything on the clipboard and he showed the befuddled inspector the door.

Chervenka had little regard for most governmental entities. Larry Mawby says Earl built a farmhouse south of town but never completed it. On purpose! He felt that if it wasn't finished, the county tax collector couldn't assess it. Earl told Larry that it worked like a charm.

Dennis Gripentrog went to see Earl about

making a new mailbox that he wanted to install on the roadside by his home. "I'd like it to be about four feet high," said Dennis. "OK," replied Earl.

"Can you make it ovular in shape?"

"Yep."

"I want a design on it that looks like climbing ivy."

"I can do it."

"And then I want you to make it appear to be about 40 years old."

With that, there was a notable pause. Earl asked Dennis, "Do you know Maisy Smith?" Dennis said he didn't. To which Earl replied, "That's her over there across the street sitting on her porch. And you're going to meet her — because I'm going to kick your ass clear over there."

One day a local came into the shop with a friend whom he introduced to Earl as one of the four or five greatest nuclear physicists in the world. Earl replied, "Hi. I'm Earl Chervenka. There's only one of me."

Truer words were never spoken.

"I'VE OFTEN WONDERED WHAT EVER HAPPENED TO THOSE PEOPLE I GAVE DIRECTIONS TO..."

# The three "r's"

**Leelanau Enterprise**, April, 1885

"Twenty new books have been added to the Leland Township Library. Let every good parent see that his child cultivates the habit of reading instead of loafing around the iron works, or pool halls of the village."

~

**Leelanau Enterprise**, October 1919

"The children of St. Mary's School
in Provemont have a two weeks
potato vacation."

**Leelanau Enterprise**, September 1895

"The new teacher has been at his post at the Bingham School for nearly two weeks and is still alive. He claims that the reports of this school being bad are greatly exaggerated."

# The jokester

The people of Northport will attest to the fact that their fellow citizen David Chrobak has a curious sense of humor. At present he owns an antique shop in the village with a large sign out in front that reads "Dead People's Stuff." Yet for decades he owned and managed the Mill Pond Inn on the northwest edge of town. It was a prominent piece of property composed of a large handsome house and expansive grounds. Because of the location, David knew he could be creative with his domain.

For years, David ran his Northport B&B in the summer and a gift/floral business in St. Thomas during the winter. In 1969, there was a "campy-craze" for plastic pink flamingos. David ordered a gross of them for his Caribbean shop, but something went haywire and the shipment arrived in Northport. He decided to put them in the yard of the Mill Pond Inn, but not all at once. He started with one, and every day or so added another. The flamingos wound around the yard and down by the pond. When the yard was filled with 144 of them, he had run out of flamingos. It pleased him that for weeks thereafter, people drove by slowly or into his driveway just to see Northport's magnificent flock of flamingos.

David seems to have a thing for birds. One day a neighbor ran over to the inn. He'd just heard a woman's hysterical scream and was alarmed. It turned out that David had recently bought a pair of peacocks. The neighbor had never before heard the birds' loud and unpleasant call. Seeing that the source of the scream was a bird relieved the neighbor, for the moment. But eventually, because peacocks do what they do, David's flock grew to six. Somehow neighbors and guests at the B&B learned to live with the noise, but strangers awakened in the middle of the night may have imagined that little sleepy Northport was a town full of womanizing fiends.

Chrobak is not a hunter and every November he is appalled at pictures in the *Enterprise* showing smiling hunters holding up the heads of their dead deer. What galls him even more is seeing deer being hauled home on car roofs. So, one year he purchased a mannequin of a woman designed to be clad in the latest styles. David didn't bother with the clothes and strapped her naked to the top of his car. He really enjoyed the shocked stares he received as he drove through town. Eventually, he was pulled over by a county deputy. "What's this all about?" asked the cop. David explained that if hunters could strap deer to their roofs, he felt he could do the same with the naked lady on his. The officer agreed that he was breaking no law, but if someone were to drive into a tree and get killed because they were gawking at David's lady, there could be serious legal consequences. After some thought, David agreed and sat down to see if he might come up with something else outrageous.

He particularly loved decorating for Christmas. One year he placed a mannequin dressed as Santa on the roofline of his inn. One of Santa's hands was on the chimney top, the other on the electric line leading to the building. At night he directed a strobe light toward Santa, which went on and off intermittently, causing traffic to stop.

He created his proudest Christmas scene a few years later. In the middle of the large yard of the Mill Pond Inn, David parked a pickup truck sideways. In front of it was positioned a wrecked sleigh. A large plastic reindeer lying on its side was lodged in the truck's snowplow. Several other reindeer were in the yard with their feet in the air. Wrapped presents were strewn across the snow. Santa, meanwhile, was up among the branches of a tree. In the spirit of the season, David added a religious touch with Mary and Joseph overlooking the carnage. Then, on Christmas morning, he produced his coup de grâce. The yard of the inn was filled with pink balloons and a sign reading, "It's a girl!"

If you ever want to know the true meaning of the term "panicked expression," simply say to any resident of Northport, "I wonder what David Chrobak has planned for the holidays."

# The sporting life

**Leelanau Enterprise**, Sept. 23, 1897

"The Baseball match Sunday afternoon in Jack Murry's field was a kind of failure on account of the rain."

⌣

Golfing in the North: In May 2005, Jerry Muir left the 18th green of his Leland golf club and immediately got his golf cart stuck in a snow drift.

⌣

**Leelanau Enterprise**, Feb. 12, 1935

"The young people of Leland formed a skating club at a formal meeting held in Leland. The name of the club is to be 'The Leland Skating Club.'"

## Wearin' of the Green

From the *Suttons Bay Courier*, March 22, 1928
Composed by Misses Mary Popp
    and Rita Hahnenberg
(Written to honor St. Patrick's Day in the village)


Oh, Paddy dear and did you hear the news
    going round,
The people of Lake Leelanau and others of
    this town,
Tod—day proclaim that they're Irish, it
    certainly can be seen
By all the fancy trimmin's and wearin's
    of the green.
Severin Belanger, who isn't very lean,
Sells hot dogs and sandwiches, the best
    you've ever seen,
He runs the Dew Drop Inn with help of
    Dan and Bean,
Today they had new sandwiches with
    shamrocks in between.
Mr. Valley owns the grocery store on the
    corner of the street
On St. Patrick's Day he has a smile for
    everyone he meets.
He has an Irish dog named Buster; today he
    could be seen,

He had round his neck a ribbon that was
   green, green, green.
There's N.J. Plamondon, he's another
   of the clan.
He sells everything that's Irish, even
   shamrocks in a can.
Harold Porter and Roy Couturier, they run
   the barber shop,
And Henry Bartenhagen is our little
   village cop.
Oscar Runge is our milk man; he's Irish
   to the core
Today he made an extra call at
   everybody's door.
I feel bigger every year, but how grand
   it all does seem,
As each St. Patrick's Day comes round, and a
   wearin' of the green.

# Angling

**Leelanau Enterprise**, Oct. 28, 1897

"Otto Mix made a fine catch of fish in Traverse Lake recently. This is not a myth, but an actual fact."

ᔪ

**Leelanau Enterprise**, Sept. 10, 1896

"Trooling [sic] for trout is now a fine sport in the bay and almost everyone is telling likely fish stories. Geo. Dame says he hooked one 6 feet long and weighs 150 pounds, more or less."

ᔪ

Some background: From the 1950s through the 1980s, an inedible trash fish named the alewife surged in the Great Lakes to the detriment of many native fish populations. The alewife, a species of saltwater herring, got into Lake Michigan through Canada's Welland Canal. It adapted poorly to fresh water, creating horrible seasonal die-offs. Beaches were fouled. To combat the problem Coho and Chinook salmon from the Northwest were introduced into Lake Michigan. It worked well. The salmon loved to gobble up alewives, and they grew to be a wonderful prize for sports fishermen. However, during the early years of the venture, the salmon headed for any inviting stream when it was time for spawning in the fall. The Leland River was no exception. Salmon jammed Fishtown's waters by the thousands, trying unsuccessfully to jump the dam. Onlookers crowded the docks. They watched in awe as the waters roiled. One fudgie saw Captain Jack Duffy and, pointing toward the river, said, "Someone told me those are freshwater porpoises. Is that true?" Without hesitation, Duffy answered, "Yes, but they are very hard to catch."

৵

During those first years of the salmon runs, Fishtown's docks overflowed with zealous seasoned fishermen as well as frantic amateurs. Lines flew in all directions. Ears and hats were hooked. Windows in the shanties were smashed by back-cast lead weights. One day the artist David Grath strolled down to take in the scene. A couple of novice anglers approached him and asked if he knew what the salmon were biting on. To this day David doesn't know why he came up with his answer, which was, "Barbie dolls." "You can get them in any toy store. Just embed a hook or two in them. There's something about the way Barbie's hair streams through the water that drives those fish crazy. They can't resist them." David credits himself for causing a run on the dolls in Traverse City. Some weeks later he was 150 miles south in Kalamazoo, where an old friend approached him on the street. "I hear the salmon fishing is great up in Leland," he said. David acknowledged that was true. "I know it sounds crazy," his friend added, "but I hear they are biting on Barbie dolls!"

Today, on the wall of the master bathroom in David's house, there is a mounted salmon with a Barbie doll hanging out of its mouth.

꒰

When Ray Kellogg's cousin was a lad, he was sitting on a bridge that spans a creek in Northport. He was fishing and having a pretty good day of it. The town character named Pete was walking to his job at the canning factory. (This was the same Pete who was blown out into the bay by the gusher that roared from the drain pipe.) His path took him across the bridge where Ray's cousin was fishing.

Pete noticed three nice brook trout in a pail beside the boy. "Fishin' good?" asked Pete. "Sure is," came the reply. "I'm going home to get my gear," said Pete, who loved to fish. "I can be late for work once in a while." Quickly the cousin summoned a pal, who crawled into a nearby downstream culvert, carrying the three caught trout. Pete returned with his pole ready for some great sport. The cousin let his line drift into the culvert. There, his pal hooked on one of the trout and gave the line two or three hefty tugs. The cousin reeled in the fish. "Boy that was quick!" exclaimed Pete. The cousin cast again, letting the line float into the culvert once more. And again, there was an instant result. "What are you using for bait?" asked Pete. "Worms," replied the kid casually. Pete changed to worms just as the cousin pulled in his third trout. "Well, that's it for me," he said as he departed whistling, leaving Pete fishless and stunned.

~

**Leelanau Enterprise**, Aug. 2, 1885

"The fish in Carp Lake have ceased biting to non-residents."

﹏

**Leelanau Enterprise**, Aug. 9, 1895

"The waters of Carp Lake are extremely low
and it is reported that the fish have been
sitting on the banks using their tails for
parasols."

﹏

The grandfather had not used his boat for several
years, but he got an urge to take his grandchildren,
10-year-old Henry and 9-year-old Sadie, out for
a day of fishing on Lake Leelanau. He felt confi-
dent that both his fishing and boating skills were
as sharp as ever. He got together his old tackle box
and three rods. He packed a lunch of their favorite
sandwiches, chips, soda pop and Oreos. In addition, he purchased a box of fat crawlers that no
respectable bass could resist.

They made their way to Stander Marine,
loaded the boat, headed out into the Leland River
and promptly went aground. With that, Henry
remarked, "When Daddy takes our boat out, he
goes on the other side of those painted posts over

there." Fortunately, a patrol boat from the county Sheriff's Department was nearby to pull them off the sand bar and into deeper water. The officer was very pleasant, although the grandfather thought he detected a slight smirk on his face as he left.

They headed out into the lake to an area where Grandpa had seen other fishing boats anchored from time to time. "I think this must be a fine spot to catch some big ones," he announced to the kids. He killed the motor, grasped the anchor and threw it in the water — only to discover that he had not tied the end of the anchor's rope to the boat. "No problem," he stated as he watched it disappear. "Drift fishing is just as good, maybe even better." The next exciting moment came when Henry hooked his thumb. Grandpa came to the rescue on that one. After an hour with no nibbles or bites, they ate their sandwiches and cookies. They were good. Suddenly, the tip of Sadie's rod bent dramatically. Excitement abounded. She cranked on the reel eagerly, only to discover she was bringing in a small tree branch. Time moved slowly. The sun was hot. The fishing was not. Then Grandpa had a brainstorm. "Come on kids," he said. "Let's head back in. I think we can save the day."

In the car, Sadie asked, "Where are we going?" "To Carlson's Fisheries in Fishtown," he answered. Once there, the grandfather bought a nice slab of smoked whitefish and had it wrapped in brown paper. Back at the children's cottage, he handed the kids the package and told them, "Run in shouting, 'Mommy! Mommy! We've got fish.' Don't say we caught fish, just we got fish." From his seat in the car he could hear their shouts followed by lots of laughter.

MORAL: IF THE PLAN SOUNDS TOO GOOD
TO BE TRUE, IT'S PROBABLY FISHY.

# Cream or sugar?

There are a bunch of coffee clubs in the county. Over time, I have had the honor and joy of frequenting half-a-dozen of them. Some meet daily, some weekly. There are no formal programs, just the talk of the day. It's said that at each gathering, folks solve all the problems of the world and create a couple of new ones. I heard an old-timer at one of them say, "You know, we have a group in Florida just like this one. Last winter we unanimously decided to stop talking about our ailments. Then we discovered we had nothing to talk about."

❧

The International Coffee Club in Leland is prominent because it was once featured on national television. The club had its beginning on March 4, 1964. Currently, on slow days, six or eight gentlemen will attend. At the height of the summer, there may be 25 or 30. It recently served its $500,000^{th}$ attendee (not cups of coffee but actual persons.) I'm not sure why the word "international" is in the title, but my guess is somebody once brought in a house guest from England or other exotic foreign locale.

In February of 1973, Charles Kuralt got wind of the Leland club. He was the television reporter known for his "On the Road" segments that appeared on the *CBS Evening News with Walter Cronkite*. His were popular, heartwarming, nostalgic vignettes that ended the newscasts. The idea of a daily coffee club meeting in the back room of the local firehouse in a tiny town in northern Michigan appealed to him. He and his film crew arrived on a frigid day, but they were warmed by the gathering, good cheer and the coffee. When the segment aired it made momentary celebrities of the members of the Leland International Coffee Club, particularly Otto Hohnke. He was an elderly man with a thick German accent. He ended Kuralt's piece by saying. "Eff you vant to know anytink about anytink, you come here." Then, after a pause, he added, "And ve don't allow no vimmen."

# Miscellany encore

**Leelanau Enterprise**, Sept. 10, 1896

(Under the heading of "Northport")

"Our village has the most churches and more societies and better-looking girls and supports a finer school than any other town in the county."

⌣

**Leelanau Enterprise**, May 24, 1945

"Clarence Cook, the well-known Michigan Public Service man of Leelanau, was busy last Thursday locating trouble on the power lines. Thursday was wash day for several county families and you can't get an electric washing machine working very well when the power is off."

**Leelanau Enterprise**, January 1894

"Mr. W. Hoolihan is helping Denny Drow in his shop. Just what he does, we do not know. But we understand he takes the place of the bellows."

# Fire! Fire!

In Suttons Bay, many folks remember when their firehouse was in the heart of the business district. The old structure is still there. It's painted red and has a cupola on the top where a bell used to hang. Today the building houses a tony, peaceful restaurant. In the old days, though, when the bell rang and the siren blared, everyone in town dropped what they were doing to watch. One afternoon such an event occurred. The engine rolled out the door with the firemen aboard, siren screaming and lights flashing. It went about 20 yards, came to an abrupt halt, then backed into the building again. Folks on the sidewalks were quite puzzled. Later they learned that although the men had remembered their helmets, axes, boots and hoses, they had forgotten to look up the address for the fire.

⌐

Jim Atkinson was a member of the volunteer fire department when an evening call came in. Smoke had been seen coming out of the new St. Mary School in Lake Leelanau. The firemen raced to the scene and entered the building. They soon determined that the source of the smoke was the art department. There they discovered a smoldering carved wooden fish resting on an active hot plate. Apparently a student had lacquered it and attempted to dry it quickly, forgetting about the fish when the school day ended. Fortunately, the firemen took care of the situation before any damage was done. Today, that charred wooden piece of art resides in a glass case in the Leland fire house — the most famous smoked fish in Leelanau County.

⁓

John K. Van Raalte was the original "Van" of Leland's iconic Van's Garage, which he opened in 1934. He was a gifted mechanic and a much-admired man. For years he was chief of the Leland Volunteer Fire Department. It was in that position that he made national news. One day, he came home for lunch and smelled smoke coming from a kitchen closet that contained the hot water heater. An ironing board had been propped against it and the top of it was on fire. Van grabbed the ironing board and smothered the flame with his handkerchief. With the crisis over, he returned the handkerchief to his pants pocket and sat down to eat.

Soon, he detected smoke coming from under the table and realized that because of the handkerchief, his trousers were on fire. He pulled them off, threw them into the kitchen sink and doused the blaze. He didn't think much about the incident until the *Enterprise* somehow got wind of it and printed the story. Then folks at the *Traverse City Record-Eagle* read it and reprinted the tale as well. That brought it to the attention of the UPI, which sent out the story nationally. The Van Raaltes received clippings of the article from friends ranging from Boston to San Francisco. It even made news in Canada: "Small Town Fire Chief Sets His Own Pants on Fire." Van took it all in stride and was actually somewhat proud of his notoriety. He later referred to it as simply, "an interesting episode."

# Long arm of the law

**Leelanau Enterprise**, Dec. 5, 1895

"The Sheriff of Frankfort came to Cedar in the still hours of the night just before dawn on the Sabbath day, and arrested Mr. Holles who is charged with having too many wives."

⤙

John Van Raalte, son of Van, was asked when he started to drive. "At age 12," he replied.

"My gosh. Being that young, didn't you have trouble with the law?"

"Not really. On occasion, at that age, I'd walk up to the sheriff's office, pick up the squad car and drive it down to the garage for an oil change. Then I'd drive it back. The sheriff never blinked."

⤙

In the 1950s, Nick Lederle could hardly wait to turn 16 so he could get his driver's license. He had studied the rules of the road carefully and endlessly practiced in his father's car. When the big birthday arrived, he marched proudly up to the sheriff's office fully prepared. There a deputy asked just one question. "You know how to drive don't you?" Nick answered, "Yes." That was his entire test, which he had just passed.

In the 1960s, an older man named Johnny lived a mile or so north of Leland. Although he had limited eyesight, he was legally blind. Most every day, Johnny would drive into town straddling the center white line. He could see that. He would park his car and, to the shock of strangers, walk across the street tapping his white cane. No one can remember Johnny ever receiving a traffic ticket.

For many years the Leelanau County Sheriff's Department was based pretty much in the center of Leland. That's where the squad cars and patrol boats on their trailers were parked. Employees often performed maintenance chores outside the building, taking advantage of the space and fresh air. On one occasion, they were painting buoys orange. They were to be placed in Lake Leelanau at the mouth of the river. At the end of the day, with the job half done, they cleaned up and capped the paint can leaving it outside for the night. The next morning, Jim Atkinson, who lives directly across the street, was surprised to find a sheriff's deputy at his door. "What's up?" he asked. "Is your son here? I'd like to talk to him," replied the officer. "Someone painted one of our patrol boats orange during the night and I'm pretty sure your kid did it." Little Adam was summoned and promptly confessed. "How did you know so quickly it was my son? asked Jim. "It wasn't hard," replied the officer, "There's a set of orange foot prints leading directly to your door."

⁓

Dave Ball remembers a wintertime in the '60s when he and a pal were driving on the ice on Lake Leelanau after dark. He figured the ice was about a foot thick, so no problem. He was going about 50 mph and having a ball. Dave headed north on the lake toward a popular public beach at Nedow's Bay. Unfortunately, as he drove near the shore, his car found a weak spot in the ice and went in nose first with the engine running and the radio playing. Luckily, Dave and his friend made it out safely. They could easily see the rear end of the car sticking out of the ice because the tail lights were still glowing. The Leland Lodge was just up the hill to the west, so dripping and cold they made their way there. They found comfort standing in front of the roaring fireplace as they tried to figure out what to do next. The logical thing was to call the sheriff, which they did. The sheriff also did what was logical by calling Van Senior and requesting he come with his tow truck. Van was able to get a hook on the car and pull it out. That's about all there is to the story. Dave received no ticket but did get a stern warning from the sheriff. He's often wondered, though, about the folks in Leland who were out on the street that night. What did they think when they saw Van towing a car making sloshing noises with beer cans bobbing up and down in the back seat and fish swimming through the steering wheel?

૮

Geno Miller laughs as he recalls a time when he and some of his buddies were partying well into the night. One of them got an idea for a good practical joke. "Let's take the sign that's south of town, the one that says 'Leland 2 miles' and put it on the pole on the north end of Suttons Bay replacing the one that reads 'Northport 12 miles.' Then we'll take that one and put it on the post south of Leland." When they heard the idea, the others thought it was smashingly funny. One of the guys even had tools in his car that could accomplish the job. Geno expressed some anxiety, saying, "What if the cops catch us?" "Don't worry," answered his buddy. "They've got to sleep sometime." So off they went into the night and took down the Leland sign with ease. They headed for Suttons Bay with part of their stolen sign sticking out of the trunk. As they turned onto M204 they were struck with horror. There, parked beside the intersection, were not one, but two squad cars. With bubble lights turning, police gave chase, pulled the boys over, and asked for an explanation. "What is that road sign doing sticking out of your car?" they asked. Geno told the officers about their plan, which was obviously a hilarious one. The deputies moved out of earshot and conferred. On their return, one put his head in the window of the car and pronounced, "Officer Mead and Officer Russell fail to see the humor." Neither did the parents of the young men when, the next morning, they had to bail their sons out of the county hoosegow.

# The hoosegow

It tells you something about the priorities of the day to learn that the first public building to be erected in Empire was the jail. It was 1895. Through the years, it was used sporadically.

Dave Taghon tells a story about the Kelly brothers, who regularly frequented the bar in Empire. They came by horse and wagon. Wisely, they had trained the horse to carry them the 2½ miles back home in the wee, small hours without any guidance from them. The Kellys were also known for occasionally "getting into stuff." On one such evening, things got so rowdy that the bartender had to call the town's constable for help. He was in bed in a deep sleep when the phone rang, but after getting the message, he hurriedly dressed and got to the bar. There, he got control of the fight and arrested the Kelly boys. He transported them to the town jail only to discover he had left the house in such a rush that he had forgotten the key for the lockup. "You boys wait right here until I get back," he told them. To the astonishment of the citizenry of Empire, the Kellys did just that.

Phil Deering says when he was young, the county sheriff had a way of scaring any kid who got picked up for mischief. He'd say, "I'm not putting you in jail, although I could. Instead I'm taking you home and when I tell your father what you did, you'll wish I'd put you in jail."

و

When Nick Lederle was a young man, he had a friend who was a perpetual hell-raiser. As a result, he was a frequent resident of the county jail. He didn't seem to mind much. The food was good. That's because the sheriff would leave the key with him so he could go down to the Bluebird to get his meals.

و

Phil Deering was a Leelanau County Commissioner for a few years. As part of his duties, he would review county records, including those from the jail. In them, he began to see a pattern. The population of the slammer increased every late autumn. In addition, the same names appeared year after year. It was a puzzle, but finally he figured it out. As cold weather approached, the "repeat offenders" would throw a brick through a window or randomly punch someone just to be incarcerated in a nice warm place and get three free squares a day. If you couldn't afford to go to Florida, the hoosegow was the next best thing.

It was Pete Carlson's custom to rise each day at 4 a.m. and prepare to head for his tug in Fishtown. His wife Rita got up at the same time to make his breakfast and pack a lunch. One early morning, after he had left, she was cleaning up the kitchen when there was a knock at the door. "That's odd," she thought. Rita opened the door to find a stranger. "May I use your telephone?" he asked. "I just broke out of jail and I think I should turn myself in." Calmly she showed him the phone and looked up the number for the sheriff. When he answered, the stranger said, "I just broke out of your jail and now that I'm out I don't know what to do with myself." "Where are you?" asked the sheriff. "Where am I?" the stranger asked Rita. "You're at the Carlson's on First Street in Leland," she answered. The stranger relayed the information. "Stay right where you are," said the sheriff. "I'll be right there." And just like the Kelly brothers of Empire, the stranger did what he was told.

142

### Leelanau Enterprise, April 1885

"About eight o'clock on Monday night, a bright light was seen, and a considerable amount of smoke was issuing from the Leelanau County jail house. Upon investigation, it was found that a prisoner, whose name was Kerzog, was seeking to make his escape by burning his way through the walls."

### Leelanau Enterprise, Nov. 27, 1930

"Theodore Rice Takes Flight ... Is Found.

Leelanau County's jail must lack some comforts to which certain of its infrequent inmates are accustomed. At any rate, Theodore Rice of Lake Leelanau was so dissatisfied that he said goodbye to the lockup twice after being placed therein by county officers. The first evening deputy sheriff William Dalton took supper to the jail for Rice, and while he was eating went outside to get wood for the fire. Jailbirds of the Leelanau County variety are not as a rule flighty and Dalton, with long experience with them, thought nothing of going out and leaving the door unlocked. This 'bird' did not run true to form, however, and when Dalton returned with his load of fuel, the former had flown.

A manhunt was at once instituted, and the next morning Rice was found at his home near Lake Leelanau, comfortably sleeping. He was herded into jail once more. This time, for greater safety, he was locked in a cell and not given the run of the jail.

All went well until Sunday evening. That's when Rice discovered that he could leave his cell by means of a hole in the bars over the door and Rice was again at liberty. Deputy Dalton noticed the direction he took, then reported to the sheriff and the manhunt was on once more. Monday, the sheriff located the fugitive and "as Rice was ill, he has been permitted to remain at the home of relatives for the present."

**Leelanau Enterprise**, Dec. 18, 1930

"Another Escape From Local Jail

Laurence Korson Departs Quietly
Tuesday Night

When prisoners get tired of the Leland jail, they leave without giving their new address. At any rate, Laurence Korson, arrested on Monday on a liquor charge, departed for unknown parts Tuesday evening. His longing for a change of scenery prompted him to remove one of the bars from a basement window and make his escape. As yet, Korson has not been found."

# Ultimate wisdom

At the beginning of this opus, I told you about my friend and his book of New England humor. I also informed you of my quest to find comic stories right here at home. After reflecting on the yarns I found, I have come to the conclusion that we have just as much to laugh about here in our small Leelanau County as our Down East brethren have in their *entire* state. And further, I think our funny stuff is most certainly better. Therefore, I have arrived at the following:

MORAL: THE REIGN OF MAINE
IS PLAINLY ON THE WANE.

## I'm Going Back to Leelanau

A Song By Harry Dumbrille
The Poet of Leelanau
1927


He went away from Leelanau,
The place he loved so well,
Out in the world's vast wilderness
A little time to dwell;
When hard times came, he packed his grip
And took the road that led
Back to his home in Leelanau,
And this is what he said:
CHORUS
I'm going back to Leelanau,
To Leelanau, my home,
I'll not again leave Leelanau
Out in the world to roam,
I'm going back to Leelanau
For happy is this lad
Who has a home in Leelanau?
I tell you I am glad.

She went away from Leelanau
To see the city's sights
To spend her time in gayety
'Mid Broadway's gleaming lights
But when her money had been spent
She took the road that led
Back to her home in Leelanau,
And this is what she said:

I'm going back to Leelanau;
'Tis Leelanau I love;
There's no place good as Leelanau
Excepting up above;
I'm going back to Leelanau
To dear old ma and dad;
To have a home in Leelanau,
I certainly am glad.

GO TO BLACK

SCOTT CRAIG is a retired television producer, direc-
tor and writer who started as a radio disc jockey, then
went on to work for NBC and CBS-owned television
stations in Chicago.

In 1975, Craig formed his own production company
and produced hundreds of documentaries for local and
national audiences. His programs appeared on CBS,
NBC, Turner, Home and Garden, Fox, and others. His
work for PBS included "Lost in America," narrated by
Hal Holbrook; two installments of Frontline; the thir-
teen-part series "On the Waterways," hosted by Jason

Robards; and the Peabody Award-winning special, "Studebaker: Less Than They Promised." For six years he produced two series for HGTV, "the Good Life" and "Extreme Homes."

After retiring, for the fun of it, he created a radio feature, "The Story Next Door," which aired on two northern Michigan stations for twelve years. In 2013, he turned his radio series into a popular book.

Scott Craig and his work have won more than one hundred awards, including a National Emmy and thirty-two Emmys from the Chicago Chapter of the Television Academy, more than anyone in the history of Chicago television.

Craig lives in Leland, Michigan, with his wife, Carol Bawden.

HENRY COLEMAN is Scott Craig's grandson. He is a recent graduate from the Wildwood School in Los Angeles. Henry devoted parts of six summers attending Interlochen Arts Camp where he studied visual arts. This fall, he will enter Parsons School of Design in New York City, where he intends to concentrate on illustration. In the future, he hopes to tell stories through his art, creating animation for the film and television industries. Henry has spent portions of every summer of his life at his family's cottage in Leland, Michigan.

Made in the USA
Monee, IL
15 June 2020